My World

In My
World

by Heather Adamson

Consulting Editor: Gail Saunders-Smith, PhD

Consultant: Susan B. Neuman, EdD
Former U.S. Assistant Secretary for Elementary
and Secondary Education
Professor, Educational Studies, University of Michigan

Mankato, Minnesota

Pebble Books are published by Capstone Press,
151 Good Counsel Drive, P.O. Box 669, Mankato, Minnesota 56002.
www.capstonepress.com

1 2 3 4 5 6 10 09 08 07 06 05

Library of Congress Cataloging-in-Publication Data
Adamson, Heather, 1974–
    In my world / by Heather Adamson.
    p. cm.—(Pebble Books. My world)
    Summary: "Simple text and photographs introduce basic community concepts
related to our world including location, things in our world, and basic facts about
other worlds"—Provided by publisher.
    Includes bibliographical references and index.
    ISBN 0-7368-4242-X (hardcover)
    1. Geography—Juvenile literature. 2. Earth—Juvenile literature. I. Title.
II. Series: My world (Mankato, Minn.)
G133.A332 2006
910—dc22   2004030961

Note to Parents and Teachers

The My World set supports national social standards related to
community. This book describes and illustrates the world. The
images support early readers in understanding the text. The
repetition of words and phrases helps early readers learn new
words. This book also introduces early readers to subject-specific
vocabulary words, which are defined in the Glossary section. Early
readers may need assistance to read some words and to use the
Table of Contents, Glossary, Read More, Internet Sites, and Index
sections of the book.

Table of Contents

My World. 5

Parts of Earth. 9

Other Worlds 17

Glossary 22

Read More 23

Internet Sites 23

Index 24

My World

My world is
the planet Earth.
Earth is shaped
like a ball.

Earth is one of
nine planets
in our solar system.
These planets
move around the Sun.

8

Parts of Earth

Earth is made of
land and water.
Earth has seven continents
and five oceans.

10

Earth has mountains, deserts, fields, and forests.

12

Earth is full of life.

Many people live on Earth.

Trees, grasses, and plants
grow on Earth.

Many animals
live on Earth. Birds fly.
Bugs crawl. Fish swim.

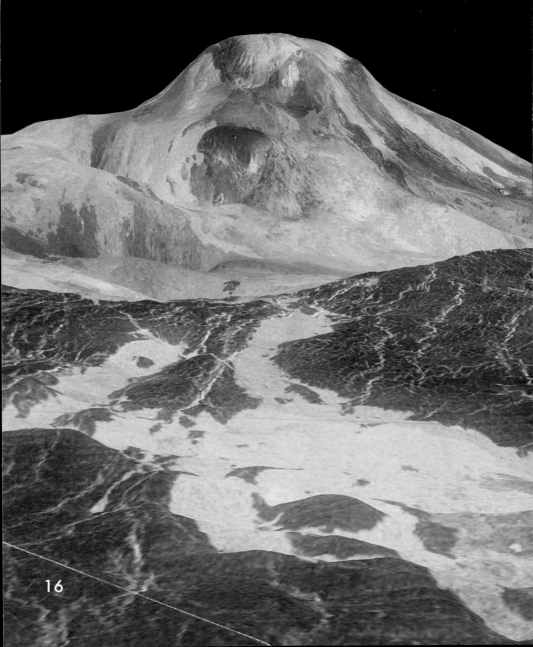

16

Other Worlds

Other planets
are not like my world.
People, plants, and
animals cannot live
on other planets.

the surface of the planet Venus

Some planets are rocky.

Mars is rocky.

Other planets are made
of gas and ice.

⬅ the surface of the planet Mars

Earth is our world.
What do you think
other worlds are like?

Glossary

continent—one of the seven main land areas of Earth

desert—an area of dry land with few plants; deserts receive very little rain.

forest—a large area covered with trees and plants

ocean—a large body of salt water

planet—a large object that moves around a star

Read More

Adamson, Thomas K. *Earth.* Exploring the Galaxy. Mankato, Minn.: Pebble Plus, 2004.

Lomberg, Michelle. *Planets.* Science Matters. Mankato, Minn.: Weigl, 2003.

Mitchell, Melanie. *Earth.* First Step Nonfiction. Minneapolis: Lerner, 2004.

Rustad, Martha E. H. *The Planets.* Out in Space. Mankato, Minn.: Pebble Books, 2002.

Internet Sites

FactHound offers a safe, fun way to find Internet sites related to this book. All of the sites on FactHound have been researched by our staff.

Here's how:

1. Visit *www.facthound.com*
2. Type in this special code **073684242X** for age-appropriate sites. Or enter a search word related to this book for a more general search.
3. Click on the **Fetch It** button.

FactHound will fetch the best sites for you!

23

Index

animals, 15, 17
continents, 9
deserts, 11
Earth, 5, 7, 9, 11,
   13, 15, 21
fields, 11
forests, 11
grasses, 13
land, 9

mountains, 11
oceans, 9
people, 13, 17
planets, 5, 7, 17, 19
plants, 13, 17
solar system, 7
Sun, 7
trees, 13
water, 9

Word Count: 120
Grade: 1
Early-Intervention Level: 12

Editorial Credits
Mari C. Schuh, editor; Juliette Peters, designer and illustrator; Jo Miller, photo researcher;
   Scott Thoms, photo editor

Photo Credits
Bruce Coleman Inc./S. Nielsen, 20 (background)
Capstone Press/Karon Dubke, cover, 1 (foreground), 4, 20 (foreground)
Comstock, 10 (upper right and lower right)
Corbis/Ecoscene/Andrew Brown, 10 (lower left); Setboun, 12
Corel, 14 (top right)
David R. Frazier Photolibrary, 10 (upper left)
NASA/Johnson Space Center, 1 (background), 8, 16, 18
Photodisc, 14 (bottom)
Stockbyte, 14 (top left)

24